A DIFFERENT KIND OF HERO

SALLY CLARKSON
JOEL CLARKSON

A *different* KIND OF *hero*

A GUIDED
JOURNEY
THROUGH
THE BIBLE'S
MISFITS

TYNDALE
MOMENTUM™

The nonfiction imprint of
Tyndale House Publishers, Inc.

Visit Tyndale online at www.tyndale.com.

Visit Tyndale Momentum online at www.tyndalemomentum.com.

Visit Sally Clarkson at www.sallyclarkson.com.

Visit Joel Clarkson at www.joelclarkson.com.

TYNDALE, *Tyndale Momentum*, and Tyndale's quill logo are registered trademarks of Tyndale House Publishers, Inc. The Tyndale Momentum logo is a trademark of Tyndale House Publishers, Inc. Tyndale Momentum is the nonfiction imprint of Tyndale House Publishers, Inc., Carol Stream, Illinois.

A Different Kind of Hero: A Guided Journey through the Bible's Misfits

Copyright © 2016 by Sally Clarkson and Joel Clarkson. All rights reserved.

Photograph of authors copyright © 2016 by Bethany Sollereder. All rights reserved.

Designed by Dean H. Renninger

Unless otherwise indicated, all Scripture quotations are taken from the *Holy Bible*, New Living Translation, copyright © 1996, 2004, 2015 by Tyndale House Foundation. Used by permission of Tyndale House Publishers, Inc., Carol Stream, Illinois 60188. All rights reserved.

Scripture quotations marked ESV are taken from *The Holy Bible*, English Standard Version® (ESV®), copyright © 2001 by Crossway, a publishing ministry of Good News Publishers. Used by permission. All rights reserved.

For information about special discounts for bulk purchases, please contact Tyndale House Publishers at csresponse@tyndale.com or call 800-323-9400.

Printed in the United States of America

22   21   20   19   18   17   16
7   6   5   4   3   2   1

CONTENTS

INTRODUCTION

"My grace is sufficient for you, for my power is made perfect in weakness." Therefore I will boast all the more gladly of my weaknesses, so that the power of Christ may rest upon me.

2 CORINTHIANS 12:9, ESV

Scripture is full of imperfect, fearful warriors and champions— men and women who didn't quite fit in or immediately stand out. In other words, it is chock-full of stories about people who aren't so very different from us. Like them, we often want to hide our differences—those tender places that set us apart from others. At other times, we wonder how we can love a family member or a friend whose struggles demand more patience or wisdom than we can drum up on our own. God's response? His strength is most available to us—and most evident—in our weakness.

This guide was written as a companion to *Different*, the book I (Sally) wrote with my son Nathan to detail our journey to understand and ultimately embrace both his strengths and his struggles. And now, rather than leaning heavily on our own story in this guided study, we invite you to journey with us into some incredible stories in the Bible. It's possible you first learned about people like Samson and Ruth from Bible stories you were told as a child, but have you ever stopped to consider just what unlikely heroes they are? You or someone you love may have been called offbeat, odd, or a little outside the box. Everyone you'll meet in *A Different Kind of Hero* was called that—or worse!

Depending on whether you want to engage with God about your struggles one on one, or whether you prefer to wrestle with difficult questions alongside others, you can complete this twelve-chapter study on your own, with a spouse or other family member, or in a small group setting. In each chapter, you'll read the story of a different hero from Scripture. Each contains

- *A brief definition* of a word that describes that person— and that could characterize anyone.* Our hope is that you'll spend a few moments considering whether you or someone you love also fits that description.
- *A passage from Scripture* that will introduce you to one of the "different" heroes God worked through, whether in ancient Israel or the early church.
- *A retelling of a key scene from that hero's life.* We've written these in a way we hope will make you feel

---

* Most of the definitions come from OxfordDictionaries.com. Some definitions at the start of chapters 5, 6, and 11 come from *Merriam-Webster's Collegiate Dictionary*, 11th edition, or merriam-webster.com.

as if you are walking alongside these people as God asks them to take a risk or to do the impossible. We are storytellers and not formal theologians, so any imaginative elements in these stories are not meant to be a statement of how each story *actually* unfolded, but rather one notion of how it *might* have played out. Though we have attempted to be painstakingly attentive to the accuracy of Scripture, we have also carefully and respectfully used imagery and dialogue that aren't explicitly stated in Scripture. Though we hope you enjoy our take on these stories, we encourage you to go back and get familiar with the source material yourself, and learn the stories straight from Scripture, as well.

- *Outside the Lines.* Each chapter ends with some additional Scripture passages and practical questions to help you contemplate what each hero has to teach you about living in the joy and strength that God offers. Notice that there's space in this section to jot down your thoughts and ideas. You can use a separate notebook or journal if you prefer.

As you take this guided journey alongside twelve biblical misfits, our prayer is that you will find new hope and direction as they point you to the One who sustained them, guided them, and never stopped loving them. After all, even today His grace and strength are unmistakable to others in the places you and I feel most vulnerable.

CHAPTER 1

Created outside the Box

*Here's to the crazy ones, the misfits, the rebels, the
troublemakers, the round pegs in the square holes.
. . . They push the human race forward, and while
some may see them as the crazy ones, we see genius,
because the ones who are crazy enough to think that
they can change the world are the ones who do.*

STEVE JOBS

Originality (noun):

1. the ability to think independently and creatively
2. the quality of being novel or unusual

*As the Ark of the LORD entered the City of David,
Michal, the daughter of Saul, looked down from her
window. When she saw King David leaping and dancing
before the LORD, she was filled with contempt for
him. . . .*

*When David returned home to bless his own family,
Michal, the daughter of Saul, came out to meet him.
She said in disgust, "How distinguished the king of Israel*

looked today, shamelessly exposing himself to the servant
girls like any vulgar person might do!"
    David retorted to Michal, "I was dancing before
the LORD, *who chose me above your father and all his*
family! He appointed me as the leader of Israel, the people
of the LORD, *so I celebrate before the* LORD. *Yes, and I*
am willing to look even more foolish than this, even to
be humiliated in my own eyes! But those servant girls
you mentioned will indeed think I am distinguished!"
So Michal, the daughter of Saul, remained childless
throughout her entire life. 2 SAMUEL 6:16, 20-23

DAVID: THE MAVERICK KING

From the beginning, David was out of the norm. As the
youngest of eight brothers, some of whom were distinguished
and well-respected in the family's social circles, he faced a
major upward climb to be noticed. When God commanded
Samuel to go to the home of Jesse to anoint one of his sons as
the next king, even the aged and venerated prophet assumed
God would choose Eliab, David's impressive-looking oldest
brother, to represent the nation of Israel. When God looked
with favor upon David, suffice it to say, his family viewed the
choice with a healthy dose of skepticism.

    Their incredulity deepened when David, still only a
shepherd guarding his father's flocks, volunteered to face off
against the Philistine giant, Goliath. Everyone around him
thought he was crazy; how could an adolescent possibly ac-

complish what a legion of soldiers had failed to do? It wasn't that David couldn't see their reasoning; through human effort and understanding, there was no way that David could ever slay the oppressive and indomitable Goliath. Yet David knew it was not by his own understanding that such feats were accomplished. God had favored him in the wilderness as he faced down lions and bears. David heard the beat of a different drummer, and that drummer was the Spirit of God.

No one could ever quite contain David; he laughed, cried, danced, expressed righteous rage, and praised God with his whole heart. He was passionate, rash, and unruly, and his impulsiveness got him into trouble many times. And yet David sought God again and again, even when he'd made major mistakes, knowing that only in God could true repentance and contentment be known.

Michal, one of David's wives, learned this the hard way. After David became king, he reclaimed the Ark of the Covenant, the joy and treasure of God's presence among the Israelites, from the pagan Philistines. He then led a celebratory procession that brought it to Jerusalem. Michal watched from a window as David returned with his army and the recaptured Ark. Bubbling over with excitement, David couldn't contain his exuberance, dancing and leaping about with unbounded joy. If that wasn't embarrassing enough, he wore a simple linen ephod that may have slipped as he was dancing. He was simply immersed in the joy of his Lord, and the happiness of God's favor on him.

When David returned home and Michal came out to see him, he was blissfully unaware of her humiliation until her fuming embarrassment spilled over in an angry rant. It wasn't fair that David should make her feel so exposed; her father, Saul, wouldn't have done such an unseemly thing. David was the king, and kings don't embarrass themselves in public, especially not in front of their subjects.

How little could she have known the hypocrisy of her own scorn; she was so blind to the presence of God that all she could see was what she was willing to see—a shameful, impolite expression by a man who just couldn't control himself.

What if, by exposing Michal to her husband's exhilaration and "improper" behavior, God was calling Michal beyond herself? What if He was giving her a chance to put aside her own sense of prudence and propriety, and instead enter in, perhaps for the first time in her life, to the foolish, crazy, unbounded joy of the presence of God? Her inability to look beyond her own expectations—the poverty of her perspective—resulted in her barrenness for the rest of her life. The unwillingness of her own soul to recognize the life of God's Spirit resulted in the void of her womb to produce human life.

Perhaps God is calling us to be more like David, and to love the Davids in our lives. It is not for us to decide whom God will use and what preconditions are necessary for His will to be done. Maybe God gives us misfits and outside-the-box family members and friends to draw us outside the safety of ourselves and into the joyous whirlwind of His glorious and beautiful plan. They may be the best models of being true to the way God designed us—with all our quirks and limitations—and the clearest examples of bringing Him honor by relying on His power in our weaknesses. Kings like David come from unlikely places and show up when we least expect it—sometimes even in our own families!

OUTSIDE THE LINES

1. *"The LORD said to Samuel, 'Don't judge by his appearance or height, for I have rejected him. The LORD doesn't see things the way you see them. People judge by outward appearance, but the LORD looks at the heart'"* (1 Samuel 16:7).

   a. Who are the misfits in your life? Are you tempted to look at them according to how others see them? What can you do to draw them out and listen to their hearts so that you don't judge them based on their outward behavior?

b. Are you a misfit yourself? In what ways do you feel people misunderstand or label you? What desires of your heart do you wish people understood better?

2. *"Now your kingdom must end, for the LORD has sought out a man after his own heart. The LORD has already appointed him to be the leader of his people, because you have not kept the LORD's command"* (1 Samuel 13:14).

a. King Saul practiced keeping up appearances and wanted to impress God, but he never sought to know God's heart. In what ways do you try to impress God? How might you, like David, offer him your heart and soul instead?

b. Sometimes what God calls us into can seem beyond our understanding or capability. Sometimes it might embarrass us or make us feel foolish. Name one or two difficult things to which you feel God may be calling you. Write a brief prayer, asking God to give you a heart for Him, as well as peace and contentment as you seek His Spirit.

3. *"David retorted to Michal, 'I was dancing before the* LORD. *. . . . He appointed me as the leader of Israel, the people of the* LORD, *so I celebrate before the* LORD. *Yes, and I am willing to look even more foolish than this, even to be humiliated in my own eyes! . . .' So Michal, the daughter of Saul, remained childless throughout her entire life"* (2 Samuel 6:21-23).

a. David was bigger than life, and his dedication to the Lord embarrassed Michal, his wife. Could it be that some of the ways the misfits in your life seem out of control might be their way of genuinely expressing a love of life or of God's fingerprints in their design?

How can you practice looking past the odd behavior and seeing the exuberant heart inside?

b. Sometimes the people or situations we think violate our sovereignty are God's way of helping us grow and let go of the things that don't matter. If you had the choice of keeping your reputation intact or of allowing God to do something special with your life, which would you choose? Explain.

CHAPTER 2

Different, Not Disabled

*A hero is an ordinary individual who finds strength to
persevere and endure in spite of overwhelming obstacles.*

CHRISTOPHER REEVE

Overcome (verb)
1. succeed in dealing with (a problem or difficulty)
2. defeat (an opponent); prevail

*The LORD told him, "I have certainly seen the oppression
of my people in Egypt. I have heard their cries of distress
because of their harsh slave drivers. Yes, I am aware of their
suffering. So I have come down to rescue them from the
power of the Egyptians and lead them out of Egypt into
their own fertile and spacious land. It is a land flowing with
milk and honey—the land where the Canaanites, Hittites,
Amorites, Perizzites, Hivites, and Jebusites now live. Look!
The cry of the people of Israel has reached me, and I have*

seen how harshly the Egyptians abuse them. Now go, for I am sending you to Pharaoh. You must lead my people Israel out of Egypt."

But Moses protested to God, "Who am I to appear before Pharaoh? Who am I to lead the people of Israel out of Egypt?"

God answered, "I will be with you. And this is your sign that I am the one who has sent you: When you have brought the people out of Egypt, you will worship God at this very mountain. . . ."

But Moses pleaded with the LORD, "O Lord, I'm not very good with words. I never have been, and I'm not now, even though you have spoken to me. I get tongue-tied, and my words get tangled."

Then the LORD asked Moses, "Who makes a person's mouth? Who decides whether people speak or do not speak, hear or do not hear, see or do not see? Is it not I, the LORD? Now go! I will be with you as you speak, and I will instruct you in what to say."

EXODUS 3:7-12; 4:10-12

MOSES: THE STUTTERING PRINCE

Moses was never much for words. Raised in the Pharaoh's court but torn between his Hebrew roots and his adoptive Egyptian culture, he struggled to find his place. Who could possibly understand him? Though a Hebrew, he had been accepted into the family of the lord of the land. Never fully an Egyptian, his adoption into this royal family cast suspicion upon him in the eyes of his own people, who were oppressed and enslaved by those who'd raised him up to a high position. Compounding this was Moses' struggle to speak clearly, an impediment worsened by the anxiety that accompanied his unusual position.

What a horrible fear must have plagued Moses. Misunderstood on all sides and lacking the ability to express himself, Moses must have felt pushed into a corner of growing frustration and anger. It caught up to him suddenly when he saw an Egyptian mercilessly beating a helpless Hebrew slave. There was no reasoning with this brute; no one ever listened to Moses anyway. In a split moment everything converged and boiled over in a fit of violent rage. When Moses stopped seeing red, he looked down to see the dead Egyptian at his feet, slain by his own hands. It didn't take long for him to realize that someone had seen him. The next day, Moses tried to break up a fight between two Hebrews, only to have the aggressor ask him whether Moses planned to kill him as he'd killed the Egyptian. What was he to do? He couldn't win by reasoning with people; his words came out like a jumbled puzzle, twisted and stripped of their meaning. Not only that, but Pharaoh wanted to kill Moses because he had murdered an Egyptian. It was hopeless; there was nothing to do but run away from this unredeemable mess.

In the wilderness, Moses finally found himself. He was no longer bound by any expectations, distrust, or ultimatums. No one would condemn him because he lacked the ability to defend himself with his words. In the desolate open spaces, there was just silence—pure, merciful silence. When Moses finally encountered civilization again, it was to rescue a gaggle of Midianite women from predatory shepherds. No need for words here; just pure action! Welcomed for his unintended heroism, Moses began again with a new people and a new life. As a shepherd for his father-in-law, he found peace, simplicity, and solitude. His days took him far away from others, far away from prying voices to which he felt entirely inadequate to respond. For the first time in many years, Moses felt truly content.

And then one day, Moses suddenly stood before a burning bush. Drawing close to this strange, unconsuming fire, Moses' treasured silence was broken, and into the silence came the voice of God. Now there was nowhere for Moses to run; he must face this deity, and he must speak. If his voice failed before kings, how much more would his voice fail before God? And then came the terrifying commission: He was to be God's mouthpiece to the new Pharaoh.

It was too much; God was asking too much of him. It was, in part, his inability to communicate clearly that had landed him here in the first place. Didn't God know that he was broken and messed up, a poor choice? His words were like a tangled web; he could never accomplish what God wanted. If only God would ask him to do a mighty deed instead; yes, that would be much better. No words; he was better with action.

Well, we know the end of the story. Not only would

Moses speak to Pharaoh with the help of his brother, Aaron, he would also perform mighty deeds—parting the Red Sea, carrying the tablets of the law down from Mount Sinai, bringing forth water from a rock in a dry desert. God didn't want an eloquent spokesperson; God wanted to express His glory through an imperfect vessel. God showed that no impossibility can stop Him and that it is for His glory and from His desire that He works through our weaknesses. In our strengths, we try to prove to God what we can do, but in our disabilities and weaknesses, God proves to us what He can do.

Did this mean that Moses never struggled with his impediment or a quick temper again? Certainly not. When he came down from the mountain to find the Israelites worshiping a golden calf, his old anger returned. God had to recast His own Ten Commandments because Moses lost his temper! That little episode in the desert where Moses brought forth water from the rock for stubborn, hard-headed, thirsty Israelites by striking it twice (see Numbers 20:2-12)? His impulsive rage cost him entry into the Promised Land. We will never be perfect before we get to heaven. But God uses vessels of clay—brittle, easily broken material—to prove His profound strength. His desire is not to make us content, but to draw us into His amazing plan for redemption.

Like Moses, we may try to run away or tune out God when He calls us to do something that we are sure is beyond us. When we follow God's leading (or even when we accept His call while kicking or screaming), we allow God's strength to be magnified by our weakness. If that is your story today, will you step out in faith and allow God to make up for your deficiencies? And if God is prompting a loved one to do the seemingly impossible, can you be like Aaron, offering the support and skills he or she needs?

OUTSIDE THE LINES

1. *"The LORD asked Moses, 'Who makes a person's mouth? Who decides whether people speak or do not speak, hear or do not hear, see or do not see? Is it not I, the LORD? Now go! I will be with you as you speak, and I will instruct you in what to say'" (Exodus 4:11-12).*

   a. What inability, disability, or weakness limits you? How does it impact your life? Make a list and write down each area that is affected by your struggle. Then pray over each of those things, asking God to enter in with His power and to be your strength where you feel weak.

   b. Have you disqualified yourself from various parts of life because of an incapacity? Ask God to give you wisdom and the courage to trust Him to work through you. Give your weaknesses to Him and ask Him to be your strength in those places where you struggle.

2. *"We now have this light shining in our hearts, but we ourselves are like fragile clay jars containing this great treasure. This makes it clear that our great power is from God, not from ourselves"* (2 Corinthians 4:7).

   a. It is easy to fall into the lie that as Christians filled with God's power, all our cracks should be sealed and we should be perfect vessels to carry the treasure of God's light within us. But maybe He wants the light to leak out and not be bottled up! What "cracks" can you surrender to God's amazing will today? How might they enable the light of God's beauty to shine through you even more brightly?

b. In what ways are you operating as if the power within you is something you must maintain and sustain on your own?

3. *"Bear one another's burdens, and so fulfill the law of Christ" (Galatians 6:2, ESV).*

a. It is easy to think that our incapacities or challenges are ours alone to bear, and yet this isn't what Scripture says. While others can't take away our ailments, they can help us carry them. God provided Aaron to help with the speaking since Moses felt so daunted by that task. In what areas of life have you tried to shoulder your burden on your own? How can you invite others to walk alongside you with those issues?

b. We were not made to be alone. We are the body
    of Christ, and we all represent different parts
    of a complete whole. Did you know that when
    one Christian suffers an impairment, limitation,
    incapacity, disability, or other challenge, we ought
    to consider that our burden as well? Just as Christ
    took on our suffering, we ought to take on others'
    suffering. With which people in your life do you
    find it difficult to relate? How might you help them
    carry their burden? If you're not sure, pray about
    how God would have you walk with them.

CHAPTER 3

Train, Don't Change

Nothing is so strong as gentleness,
nothing so gentle as real strength.

SAINT FRANCIS DE SALES

Fortitude (noun)

1. courage in pain or adversity

Samson prayed to the LORD, "Sovereign LORD, remember
me again. O God, please strengthen me just one more
time. With one blow let me pay back the Philistines for
the loss of my two eyes." Then Samson put his hands on
the two center pillars that held up the temple. Pushing
against them with both hands, he prayed, "Let me die
with the Philistines." And the temple crashed down on the
Philistine rulers and all the people. JUDGES 16:28-30

SAMSON: THE REBELLIOUS WARRIOR

The Spirit of the Lord was upon him. Samson had known it from a young age. God had bestowed unusual might upon the young man, and he used that power to its full extent. God had prepared Samson to lead his people, and the favor of God was upon him. Samson knew this in theory, but the strength itself often became Samson's focal point.

Such might set Samson apart from those around him. At times this made him feel powerful and respected; for most of his life, however, it made him feel distant from his peers, unable to interact with them as friends in the way they related to one another. As a child, he was awkward and painfully shy. His hair, left uncut as a sign of his dedication to the Lord as a Nazirite, was ragged and wild, no matter how his mother tried to tame it. His strength, which would serve him well in his adulthood, was unwieldy in his youth; another child would taunt him for his looks, and before he knew it, the bully would be laid out flat by an unintentionally forceful push by Samson. Other parents tried to be understanding when such incidents happened, knowing God's special dispensation for Samson; at the same time, they refused to let their own children spend too much time with him. Samson's parents tried to remind him that God had made him as he was for a purpose; that God desired that Samson commit his life to Him and trust Him to work things out. But as time would tell, Samson was fixated on his physical might and how it affected his life, rather than on finding God's perfect will and using his might for good.

As Samson grew older, his strength, which may have been a disadvantage in his interaction with others as a child, became a tool Samson used to accomplish his desires. He liked to think that people had learned to respect him for his power, while in fact they simply feared him. Samson's parents recognized their son's growing tendency to insist on his own way and tried to stem the tide when he demanded they arrange for his marriage with a Philistine woman, but they, too, were rebuffed by Samson's quick temper and his unyielding heart. When he wanted something, he got it, or if he didn't, he usually destroyed the person who stood in his way.

After all, if God was favoring him with His strength, Samson thought, then what of those who defied him? Yes, there was the unfortunate incident with his wife; yes, she and her father ended up being burned alive, and yes, by the time everything was over, a thousand Philistines were dead. But that was what happened when people stepped in the way of the Lord's anointed. So what if the whole incident started because he couldn't keep a secret and gave away the answer to a riddle upon which an immense bet was placed? He had been blessed with power from above, so it was best not to think too much about the times he'd misused it.

Eventually, Samson used his unchallenged might to rise to power and reign for twenty years as a judge over all of Israel; as he reached middle age, he seemed all but invincible. His identity had become so wrapped up in his gift that he began to lean on it to resolve any issues caused by his own moral indiscretions.

At the urging of Philistine's rulers, Samson's love interest, Delilah, finally discovered the secret to Samson's strength. Tired of her badgering him about the source of his strength, Samson relinquished the secret to the strength God had given to him, the blessing that had taken him to such lofty heights: his wild, uncut hair. After lulling him to sleep, Delilah called in a man who shaved off his hair. God's blessing finally slipped away from him, and he was made as weak as any common man.

Imprisoned by the very foes whose countrymen he had slain by the thousands, Samson finally understood. His strength was not what made him powerful; it was God's blessing upon him that gave him the ability to do great works. He had abused that blessing too often, using it for his own selfish means, and as a consequence, his might had been taken away from him.

The Philistines captured him, gouged out his eyes, bound him in chains, and imprisoned him. With his mighty gift now gone, he cried out to the Lord to give him one last chance to prove his worthiness and pay back the Philistines. He knew he was not worthy to bear such righteous strength, but he hoped to fulfill the work the Lord had given him to do: Strike down the Philistines. God granted him that request, and with Samson's last breath, he brought down the temple of the Philistines on thousands of them, striking a powerful blow against the enemies of God.

Whether Samson's unusual might was a rare gift or an impediment, God ultimately judged him according to how he responded to what he'd been given. When children struggle with being different, what they need to know is that God created them with the intent to tell a good story through their lives. While they may always have challenges, only they can choose to trust God and do the right thing. Those who have physical power can be shown how to use it with care and consideration; those without it can choose to live with strength of character instead.

OUTSIDE THE LINES

1. *"This is what the LORD says to Zerubbabel: It is not by force nor by strength, but by my Spirit, says the LORD of Heaven's Armies" (Zechariah 4:6).*

   a. In what areas are you tempted to try to overcome the challenges in your life through your own strength? God is able to take you far beyond what you yourself can accomplish. List the problems you are attempting to overcome without God's help and submit them into His hands.

b. Are you growing weary with the challenges in your life? Write a brief prayer asking God to give you strength. With His power within you, you will be able to overcome any obstacle.

2. *"Unless the LORD builds a house, the work of the builders is wasted. Unless the LORD protects a city, guarding it with sentries will do no good" (Psalm 127:1).*

a. What life challenge weighs on you most heavily right now? Whether it's raising your child, dealing with a difficult family member, or growing in some area yourself, where will you find the wisdom you need?

b. Whether you or your children have particular strengths or difficulties, God is the one who builds the "house" of your life. What steps can you take today to encourage you or your children to begin to see how God might work through you to help others and draw them to Him?

3. *"You must love the L*ORD *your God with all your heart, all your soul, all your mind, and all your strength"* (Mark 12:30).

a. Samson's training may have focused on his behavior without reaching his heart. How can you reach the hearts of those around you, no matter what challenges and gifts they have?

b. Our skills and talents can become hindrances if they are not used in submission to God's guidance in all areas of our lives. How closely are you following the Spirit as you use your abilities? How could you better demonstrate your love for Him through the gifts you've been given?

CHAPTER 4

How to Love the Difficult Person

We come to love not by finding a perfect person, but by learning to see an imperfect person perfectly.

SAM KEEN

Forbearance (noun)

1. patient self-control; restraint and tolerance
2. the action of refraining from exercising a legal right, especially enforcing the payment of a debt

I am boldly asking a favor of you. I could demand it in the name of Christ because it is the right thing for you to do. But because of our love, I prefer simply to ask you. Consider this as a request from me—Paul, an old man and now also a prisoner for the sake of Christ Jesus.

I appeal to you to show kindness to my child, Onesimus. I became his father in the faith while here in prison. Onesimus hasn't been of much use to you in the past, but now he is very useful to both of us. I am sending him back to you, and with him comes my own heart.

I wanted to keep him here with me while I am in these chains for preaching the Good News, and he would have helped me on your behalf. But I didn't want to do anything without your consent. I wanted you to help because you were willing, not because you were forced. It seems you lost Onesimus for a little while so that you could have him back forever. He is no longer like a slave to you. He is more than a slave, for he is a beloved brother, especially to me. Now he will mean much more to you, both as a man and as a brother in the Lord.

PHILEMON 1:8-16

ONESIMUS: THE PRODIGAL SERVANT

Philemon was a changed man. Ever since meeting the apostle Paul and subsequently encountering Jesus Christ, Philemon had clung to grace. His life had been transformed as he followed the teachings of the Nazarene, and he desired to put every element of his life under the lordship of this King. He ordered his household according to this new understanding, and he quickly became a leader in the local church in Colosse. He bowed his knee to Jesus in all parts of his life.

But Onesimus—he was a different matter altogether. He had always been difficult.

Still, after his conversion, Philemon tried to change his

ways toward everyone around him, including Onesimus. He knew that in the Kingdom of Heaven, all were equal before God. As he submitted to the will of the Holy Spirit, he was amazed at how God softened his heart toward many people in his life. He quickly became known for his generous and gentle spirit toward others.

Everyone—except Onesimus.

Philemon had tried at first; though he had often been harsh to Onesimus in the past, he thought maybe a conciliatory attitude would change things. Perhaps what was needed was a softer touch. When that didn't work, Philemon tried admonishing him with the fatherly authority that belonged to him as Onesimus's master. It was right and good that Onesimus was an indentured servant; he couldn't be trusted to make his own decisions and be mature.

Nothing seemed to work; finally Philemon decided there was nothing else he could do. He wasn't going to waste any more time trying to help Onesimus if he wasn't even going to try to act reasonable. He would put his foot down when needed to knock his servant back into line, and that would be the end of it.

Naturally, Philemon wasn't surprised when one morning he awoke to find that Onesimus had flown the coop—along with some household supplies and money. What did surprise Philemon was the letter he received from Paul, his mentor in Christ, not long after. As he read through the opening lines, he was outraged to read that Onesimus had fled to Paul, who was now sheltering him. *Of course he would go to Paul;*

he knew that Paul would be easy on him. To make things even worse, Paul reported that Onesimus had come to faith in Christ and was now asking *him*, Philemon, a godly, upstanding man, to forgive Onesimus and take him back.

Philemon stopped reading the letter and sighed deeply. Perhaps he could begrudgingly agree to take back Onesimus; but there would have to be consequences. It didn't matter if Paul thought Onesimus had repented and changed; there had to be a reckoning for all the ways in which Onesimus had embarrassed Philemon, had flaunted his kindness, and had rebelled against the right order of his household. Philemon read on, and what he saw next made him nearly jump out of his seat in anger.

Paul had the nerve to suggest that Onesimus, as a redeemed son of God, ought to be received back as a *brother*. How could Paul suggest such a scandalous thing? Not only had Onesimus done nothing to merit such an honor, it would turn the rules of his household upside down. *Philemon* was the master, and *he* deserved to decide who was honored and who was not. Perhaps there was some sort of equality before Christ in this new Kingdom, but Onesimus was rebellious, and Philemon had to maintain order in his household. Onesimus, by all accounts, had done nothing to deserve such a radical extension of friendship.

Then Philemon saw Paul's next words. "If he has wronged you in any way or owes you anything, charge it to me. . . . And I won't mention that you owe me your very soul!" (verses 18-19). Philemon turned beet red and bowed his head in shame. What a horrible hypocrite he had been; he had held Onesimus to a standard to which God had never held him. Philemon had been an idol worshiper, an adulterer, and a sham before encountering Jesus; and yet when Paul met Philemon, he didn't judge him for his pagan ways. He simply shared the kindness of Christ with him and showed him the way to new life. Through Paul's witness of the gospel, Philemon had been brought out of the mire of his own sin and set in a high place. He'd been given grace after grace. What reckoning had God ever required of him? Nothing! And yet Philemon had made *himself* the judge of hearts, required for *himself* that Onesimus atone for his sin, a burden that Christ had already satisfied on the cross.

He hesitated a moment; what if Onesimus reverted to his sinful ways? What if he fell into sin again? Philemon reflected on the multitude of ways that he himself had been forgiven, even in that very moment, for his hypocrisy toward Onesimus. There was no limit to God's forgiveness of him; how could he put a limit on the number of times he would forgive Onesimus, or anyone else?

In welcoming back Onesimus, Philemon encouraged a young man who, tradition says, went on to become a leader in the early church and was eventually martyred for his faithful service to God. By submitting his desires and his rights, Philemon changed the very face of Christian history. What if we are meant to do the same? What if in choosing to always extend grace and forgiveness to those who hurt us most, we are allowing a great work of God to come into being?

OUTSIDE THE LINES

1. *"You are all children of God through faith in Christ Jesus. And all who have been united with Christ in baptism have put on Christ, like putting on new clothes. There is no longer Jew or Gentile, slave or free, male and female. For you are all one in Christ Jesus"* (Galatians 3:26-28).

   a. What does this passage say about recognizing the value in all redeemed people, no matter where they have been or who they have been in the past?

   b. Is there anyone in your life whom you are not treating as a brother or sister in Christ? What are one or two simple ways you can change your heart toward this person?

2. *"Make allowance for each other's faults, and forgive anyone who offends you. Remember, the Lord forgave you, so you must forgive others. Above all, clothe yourselves with love, which binds us all together in perfect harmony" (Colossians 3:13-14).*

   a. Why are we commanded to forgive? Do you think forgiveness is necessary if we are to "clothe [ourselves] with love"? To be found "together in perfect harmony"? Why or why not?

   b. Who is the Onesimus in your life—someone who is difficult to nurture, to forgive—maybe even to love, at times? What about that person frustrates you most? How might you make allowance for that person's faults in such a way that you model Christ's love to him or her?

3. *"Wait patiently for the* LORD. *Be brave and courageous. Yes, wait patiently for the Lord"* (Psalm 27:14).

   a. Sometimes being brave means waiting on God for many years. How can you grow in your trust as you watch faithfully for God to work?

   b. Being strong is a choice of our will as we ask God to increase our faith. How have you or someone you know become stronger by waiting on God to act?

CHAPTER 5

The Invisible Battles of the Mysterious Mind

In the long run, we shape our lives and we shape ourselves. The process never ends until we die. And the choices we make are ultimately our own responsibility.

ELEANOR ROOSEVELT

Resourceful (adjective)
1. having the ability to find quick and clever ways to overcome difficulties
2. capable of devising ways and means

[Naomi and Ruth] continued on their journey. When they came to Bethlehem, the entire town was excited by their arrival. "Is it really Naomi?" the women asked.

"Don't call me Naomi," she responded. "Instead, call me Mara, for the Almighty has made life very bitter for me. I went away full, but the LORD has brought me home empty. Why call me Naomi when the LORD has caused me to suffer and the Almighty has sent such tragedy upon me?"

So Naomi returned from Moab, accompanied by her daughter-in-law Ruth, the young Moabite woman. They arrived in Bethlehem in late spring, at the beginning of the barley harvest.

Now there was a wealthy and influential man in Bethlehem named Boaz, who was a relative of Naomi's husband, Elimelech.

One day Ruth the Moabite said to Naomi, "Let me go out into the harvest fields to pick up the stalks of grain left behind by anyone who is kind enough to let me do it."

Naomi replied, "All right, my daughter, go ahead." So Ruth went out to gather grain behind the harvesters. RUTH 1:19–2:3

RUTH: THE PERSISTENT DAUGHTER

It was all so easy when they started out. Ruth remembered her first encounter with Mahlon; he was an Israelite, wandering with his family through Moab as a stranger. As Ruth helped introduce Mahlon to her land and the customs of her people, something about him drew her to him—and to his family. She found out that they had left Judah for Moab in the midst of a famine. She learned about Elimelech, Mahlon and Kilion's father, who had been serious about providing for his family until his untimely death soon after they arrived in Moab. And of course, there was Naomi.

During those early years, Naomi was a dear and trusted friend to Ruth. Even though she grieved the loss of her husband, Naomi, whose name meant "my joy," was a confident woman, full of grace; no doubt Ruth admired her elegance and the charm that adorned her matriarchal authority over the tending of her home. By observing Naomi, Ruth learned how to be a good wife, how to bring forth beauty and give life to those around her. It was through Naomi that Ruth first encountered true spirituality; not in the worship of inanimate idols, like the ones her own people bowed down to, but through an encounter with the living God of these Judeans.

And then without warning, everything fell apart. Naomi's sons, the bulwark of the family after Elimelech's death, both passed away suddenly, leaving the women of the family on their own.

Ruth, swimming in the sea of her grief, looked to her mother-in-law for comfort. But Naomi had changed; where before there was strength, now there was fear. In the past, Ruth could always count on the joy of Naomi's fellowship and empathy. Now Naomi was lost, cast behind a veil of grief. The light was gone from her eyes; in its place was an inexplicable wall of despair.

Every dream of Ruth's heart had morphed into a nightmare. Even the mother-in-law who had been her strength had become inaccessible. What else was there for her? She no longer considered herself a Moabite; there was nothing left for her in her land. She had made a covenant with Elimelech's family. How could she abandon this woman who had brought her into the light, even as that same woman was walking through the valley of death? She couldn't possibly know whether Naomi would ever emerge from the fog of her sorrow. It didn't matter; she would follow Naomi as the elderly woman traversed back to Bethlehem.

The journey to Judea wasn't easy, and the entry into Judean culture was even more difficult. Naomi, the only touchpoint for Ruth with this strange new culture, had changed; once a woman of profound strength, she had become a hollow shell of herself. Her hair was untended and her clothes disheveled. Her eyes, once filled with the light of life, were void and distant.

"Is that Naomi? Surely not; it can't be! What happened to you?" Ruth quickly became used to the odd looks and the suspicious glances from strangers, which were surely aimed in part at her. Who was this Moabite, and what had she done to bring back Naomi in such a state? Sometimes, in response to the questions, Naomi would reply angrily, "I am no longer Naomi. Now all I am is bitterness." Passersby would look embarrassed, rushing their children along away from this crazed woman.

The hardest thing was the pain Ruth saw in Naomi. She knew her mother-in-law was in anguish, but she felt so helpless to know how to reach her. Those first few weeks were a time of suffering with Naomi in her darkness. Finally, Ruth decided to act.

She knew Naomi couldn't pull herself out of the mire, so Ruth would receive no help from Naomi. She decided it was her responsibility to take care of herself so she could provide for Naomi until her mother-in-law could function again. Near their home, harvesters were working in a field owned by a wealthy man named Boaz. Ruth decided she would go out, like other young women, and gather any stalks that were left behind.

Through that action of intentionality, Ruth's life began to gain positive motion. Soon God would open the opportunity for her to grow in a relationship with Boaz, and Ruth's persistent hopefulness would even draw Naomi out of her dark isolation. After Ruth and Boaz's love bloomed into marriage, Naomi cared for their firstborn son, Obed, as if he were her own. Her heart, once emptied by grief, was full again.

Do you feel trapped in the mire of someone else's depression? Are the inner mental workings of someone you love confusing and disorienting? When trying to understand the mental struggles of our family members, it is so easy to allow them to set the tone of our hearts and become filled with confusion and frustration. Sometimes, instead of trying to comprehend or fix their problems, the best thing we can do is to bear with them patiently, praying for their healing, while at the same time pursuing a stable, healthy life of our own. Sometimes, choosing to be healthy even in the midst of the poor decisions of those around you is the most powerful weapon against chaos. You have the power, given to you by the Holy Spirit, to cling to hope. You have the power to do what is necessary to create spaces that allow you to breathe, be restored, and enjoy life.

Today love those who struggle with mental issues by helping yourself so that you can support them in their time of need.

OUTSIDE THE LINES

1. *"We know that God causes everything to work together for the good of those who love God and are called according to his purpose for them" (Romans 8:28).*

    a. If God works everything for the good of those who love Him, what are areas of your life in which you are tempted to despair? How can you look at your circumstances through God's eyes?

    b. It's natural to expect a certain story for our lives from God, and it can be surprising and discouraging when we end up with difficult long-term challenges. His power at work in us isn't altered by what appear to be unchangeable situations. What challenges in your life feel insurmountable today? How could committing them to Jesus, the great storyteller, change your outlook on them?

2. *"God blesses those who patiently endure testing and temptation. Afterward they will receive the crown of life that God has promised to those who love him"* (James 1:12).

    a. It's easy to feel as if our current circumstances are the whole truth of our lives, but God has an eternal perspective. How does this verse provide you with hope for your own situation?

    b. What are the temptations pressing on you right now as you try to be faithful and endure? Write down the things that are pulling you away from waiting on God.

3. *"We can rejoice, too, when we run into problems and trials, for we know that they help us develop endurance. And endurance develops strength of character, and character strengthens our confident hope of salvation. And this hope*

will not lead to disappointment. For we know how dearly God loves us, because he has given us the Holy Spirit to fill our hearts with his love" (Romans 5:3-5).

a. Growing in character is a dance between you and the Holy Spirit. It involves both being strong and resting in God's grace when you don't feel strong. Do you see your endurance growing as you love a person who is struggling? If so, how? If the situation currently leaves you feeling hopeless, what does God's promise to fill your heart with His love mean to you?

b. It's easy to feel in the moment like nothing will ever change. But God's hope doesn't disappoint. God sees the whole story, and He's right in the middle of it with you right now. Take a few moments to consider a struggle you've faced in the past week. How did God show up to support or guide you? It might have been as simple as a chance encounter with someone who offered help or an encouraging word.

CHAPTER 6

Why Me, God?

But there was no need to be ashamed of tears,
for tears bore witness that a man had the
greatest of courage, the courage to suffer.

VIKTOR E. FRANKL

Long-suffering (adjective)

1. suffering a long time without complaining

2. patiently enduring lasting offense or hardship

Then the LORD said to Job,

> *"Do you still want to argue with the Almighty?*
> *You are God's critic, but do you have the answers?"*

Then Job replied to the LORD,

> *"I am nothing—how could I ever find the answers?*
> *I will cover my mouth with my hand.*

> *I have said too much already.*
> *I have nothing more to say."*

Then the LORD answered Job from the whirlwind:

"Brace yourself like a man,
because I have some questions for you,
and you must answer them.

"Will you discredit my justice
and condemn me just to prove you are right?

Are you as strong as God? . . .

Then Job replied to the LORD:

"I know that you can do anything,
and no one can stop you.

You asked, 'Who is this that questions my wisdom
with such ignorance?'
It is I—and I was talking about things I knew
nothing about,
things far too wonderful for me.

You said, 'Listen and I will speak!
I have some questions for you,
and you must answer them.'

I had only heard about you before,
but now I have seen you with my own eyes.

I take back everything I said,
and I sit in dust and ashes to show my
repentance."

JOB 40:1-9; 42:1-6

JOB: THE SUFFERING FATHER

Standing in the ashes of his old homestead, Job reflected on his long and torturous journey. He recalled seeing the remains of his once-fruitful land and the place where his children had died. He felt empty, devoid of even the spark of light. Everything that had been his had been taken from him, and he and his wife were left to face the dark future alone.

At first, he repeated the words he felt were appropriate. "The LORD gave, and the LORD has taken away; blessed be the name of the LORD" (Job 1:21, ESV). It was the right thing to say, but it felt so unsatisfactory, so indefensible. He wanted to die, to disappear into the earth and never return to the light of day; but even this was denied him. He must do nothing but simply survive, awaiting something; what, he couldn't say.

It didn't take long for his friends to show up, and he hoped for comfort and fellowship from these trusted companions. For the first seven days, they sat with him silently, their consolation evident in their simple presence. When they started talking to him, however, Job found out firsthand how quickly friends can become faithless. Rather than encouraging him, they confronted him. Surely, they said, his suffering came because he'd done something against the Lord. They told him that God must be judging him for his sin. Job needed to confess that sin, they said, if he wanted God's blessing again. At first Job could not believe his friends' words; he had always tried to be a righteous man, committing all his ways to the Lord. They knew this about Job; in fact, they'd always looked up to him as an example of a man of great character. Now they were rewriting their own narrative of him, re-creating him as a man of loose morals who had offended God so greatly that the Lord had taken the drastic step of killing his entire family and destroying his livelihood.

Job would have none of this; he was a good man and had lived according to the law of God. He could not accept that the Lord would harm an innocent man so completely. God needed to provide answers; He needed to show Job why this was happening. It wasn't fair or right. How could he, a man of faithful goodness, be allowed to suffer so much? That question gnawed at Job day in and day out. Finally, he demanded that God give an answer for his suffering.

To his surprise, God did respond. And the answer He gave Job was different from what he could have ever expected. He gave Job a glimpse of what few men are able to see, the vastness and glory of creation, and God's powerful hand within it. He asked if Job could possibly give an account of the world, and all that it contains, or of the heavenly places, and all that happens in those realms. Suddenly, Job found himself in the hot seat, facing God's questions, which were far beyond Job's knowledge.

Humbling himself before God, Job accepted that he might simply be unable to understand certain things. He recommitted his life to God, repenting even in the midst of "dust and ashes."

Not only did God accept that prayer, He blessed Job with twice as much as he had before. Job looked out on his restored fortune: godly children, fields of great harvest, bounty, and goodness beyond his imagination. No doubt he was able to say again from a full heart, "The LORD gave, and the LORD has taken away; blessed be the name of the LORD."

Do you find yourself in dire circumstances beyond your control? Are you striving with God, trying to understand how He could allow such suffering? You have good company in Job. And yet, as with Job, sometimes trying to comprehend the whys of our lives is a futile process that only brings us more grief. Sometimes peace is found when we simply rest in God's goodness and leave the big questions to Him. He is our Father and our comforter. He is over all and sees us in our time of trial. His vision goes far beyond ours, and even though we may not understand why we must endure difficulty, God is faithful to guide us through it.

God's promises are true: Just as God restored Job's fortunes and gave him a joyous family beyond his wildest dreams, we can trust that God will be good to us. Tragedy is a painful wound that the world gives to all of us in time; despair is a self-inflicted injury that refuses to heal because it rejects the Healer. When we let go of our need to control and understand, we are giving ourselves into the hands of the One who can make us whole again, despite all our wounds.

OUTSIDE THE LINES

1. *"Even when I walk through the darkest valley, I will not be afraid, for you are close beside me. Your rod and your*

staff protect and comfort me. . . . Surely your goodness and unfailing love will pursue me all the days of my life, and I will live in the house of the LORD forever" (Psalm 23:4, 6).

a. Scripture acknowledges that we will face times of deep difficulty and sadness, but it also promises that God will never leave us. How have you seen evidence of that in the past week?

b. What are the fears that plague you? God wants to comfort you and take them away. Later in the Psalms, David writes that "even the darkness is not dark" to God (139:12, ESV); He is right at the center of your hurt. What situation feels so dark that you are longing for God's illumination?

2. *"He heals the brokenhearted and bandages their wounds"*
   (Psalm 147:3).

   a. At times you may feel that your suffering is invisible.
      Note, however, that the psalmist portrays a God who
      is not only sympathetic, but who actively engages
      with us in our hurt. Describe the areas of your life
      that feel most broken, and ask God to heal those
      specific wounds.

   b. Psalm 147 begins and ends with the proclamation
      "Praise the LORD!" Based on verse 3, why do the
      brokenhearted have reason to praise God? Write
      out a brief prayer thanking God for who He is and
      how He has been meeting you in your situation. If it
      feels as if He is absent, acknowledge this even as you
      claim the promise above.

3. *"Since we have a great High Priest who has entered heaven, Jesus the Son of God, let us hold firmly to what we believe. This High Priest of ours understands our weaknesses, for he faced all of the same testings we do, yet he did not sin. So let us come boldly to the throne of our gracious God. There we will receive his mercy, and we will find grace to help us when we need it most" (Hebrews 4:14-16).*

   a. In this passage God tells us to be bold in asking Him for help with our struggles, and not to be afraid to ask Him for whatever it is we need. Jesus has himself suffered and overcome, and He wants to help us overcome too. Are there areas of your life you feel are off limits to God's redemption? Identify these, and commit them to God.

b. God knows that we are weak and that we can't overcome trials and temptations on our own. Rather than living with self-condemnation over our failures and weaknesses, how does God want us to respond when we are knocked down by difficulty?

CHAPTER 7

Owning the Song Inside You

*People, even more than things, have to be restored, renewed,
revived, reclaimed, and redeemed; never throw out anyone.*

AUDREY HEPBURN

Redemption (noun)

1. the action of saving or being saved from sin, error,
   or evil
2. the action of regaining or gaining possession of
   something in exchange for a payment, or clearing
   a debt

*Before the spies went to sleep that night, Rahab went up
on the roof to talk with them. "I know the LORD has
given you this land," she told them. "We are all afraid of
you. Everyone in the land is living in terror. For we have
heard how the LORD made a dry path for you through the
Red Sea when you left Egypt. And we know what you did*

to Sihon and Og, the two Amorite kings east of the Jordan
River, whose people you completely destroyed. No wonder
our hearts have melted in fear! No one has the courage to
fight after hearing such things. For the LORD your God
is the supreme God of the heavens above and the earth
below.

"Now swear to me by the LORD that you will be kind
to me and my family since I have helped you. Give me
some guarantee that when Jericho is conquered, you will
let me live, along with my father and mother, my brothers
and sisters, and all their families."

"We offer our own lives as a guarantee for your safety,"
the men agreed. "If you don't betray us, we will keep our
promise and be kind to you when the LORD gives us the
land. . . ."

So Joshua spared Rahab the prostitute and her relatives
who were with her in the house, because she had hidden
the spies Joshua sent to Jericho. And she lives among the
Israelites to this day.

JOSHUA 2:8-14; 6:25

RAHAB: THE UNLIKELY RESCUER

Regret. It was at the heart of Rahab's life, the very lens
through which she saw her world. Regret about the choices
that had led her to her current lifestyle, a woman of the
night; regret that instead of honor, she had brought disgrace
to her family. She regretted that she had only ever truly

learned one song, and that was the song she sang to draw strangers, unknown men, into the void of her indignity. She felt trapped, locked in a cycle that couldn't be broken, giving away her pride to provide for her family. Living in Jericho meant protection from the outside world, from tribal invaders, and from the terrors of war; and yet to Rahab, the walls were those of a prison, pushing in upon her. Her home was crafted into the very sides of those great walls, her windows looking out on the breathtaking expanse of Canaan. The very beauty of the verdant landscape was like a knife in her heart, and the sight of it reminded Rahab of a life she would never have. She had learned to sing the song of regret with deft clarity, understanding its nuances and melodic twists and turns, and as she sang, her regret slowly morphed into despair.

She had heard about the coming of the Israelites while shopping in the market. Everyone was abuzz with the onslaught of this group of ragtag warriors; by now, news of the ravaging of mighty Egypt by this unlikely nomadic people had reached all of Canaan. Rumors of a strange and powerful deity who went before these Israelites filled the people of Jericho with fear. Rahab heard and scoffed. *Let them come*, she thought. Perhaps her suffering would finally be laid to rest. Perhaps the gods would be more forgiving to her in the afterlife than her own people had in this life. She was an outcast, despised; what more harm could the conquest of her city cause her than she had already experienced in a lifetime of darkness?

Then one evening she saw two men standing inconspicuously in the shadows near her door. This was not surprising to her, though it seemed rather early for such unseemly men to loiter while the sun still lingered in the western sky. She quickly invited them in and shut the door behind her, hoping no one had seen them in the street. She turned to the strangers and gave her price, and warned them to be away before the morning light. And yet, even as she spoke, she knew these were not normal customers. The light in their eyes was not that of self-interest and indulgence but of curiosity, concern, and keen awareness. As they spoke to her, she quickly apprehended their true meaning; they were spies from the camp of the Israelites, come to scout the city.

The idea of it filled her with excitement and terror all at once; at that very moment, she was committing treason against her people, a crime worthy of her own death and perhaps also the deaths of her family members. How could she keep these men while her family was in danger? Another thought quickly overtook her first fears: What life was there for her, or for her family? Could this be her salvation? She could barely hope for such a result; even if she helped these men, what good could come of it? Would Israel give any allowances to a foreign harlot?

As she continued to brood, a loud rap resounded from her front door. "Open in the name of the king!" shouted a loud and curt voice. So someone *had* seen them in the alley outside. *Just my luck*, she thought. Before she had time to mull it over, she quickly led her guests onto the roof, where she covered them with flax in a makeshift hiding spot. The banging on the door became louder. She ran and opened the door, where an imposing royal guard leered down at her suspiciously. He commanded her to give up the spies that had come to her home. She quickly improvised, responding that she didn't know who the men were, but they had taken an early leave to get out of the city before the gates closed. The guard cursed and barked orders to his men to head toward the city gate to see if they could catch up with these foreigners. Rahab closed the door behind her and breathed a sigh of relief. In an ironic twist, her reputation as a woman too familiar with men protected her from suspicion that might otherwise have resulted in a search of her home.

When she returned to the strangers on the roof, her heart beat faster and faster. She knew she was in deep now; there was only one way out, and that was to lean on the mercy of these spies. She knew the ways of the people in Canaan: unforgiving, harsh, and cruel. These men could easily betray her and leave her for dead, or even worse, in the hands of the authorities of Jericho. Whether by the sword of the Israelites or by the sword of Jericho, she felt certain that the only way forward was death and destruction for her family. But what if she could learn a new song, start anew with these strange, unknown people? She counted on this last hope; she laid out her conditions, and the Israelites, to her great surprise, accepted. They would spare the lives of Rahab and her family when they sacked the city.

The waiting was the hardest part, and when the battle was over, her city was in ruins. And yet, true to their promise, the Israelites rescued her and her whole family, bringing them to a new life. God took her broken melody and used it, not only to help the Israelites triumph over Jericho, but to redeem her song, reharmonizing it into something beautiful.

Our challenging and difficult children may also feel regret, failure, frustration, and anger. They, too, may feel like their song is broken. What if, instead of trying to make them sing the same refrain as everyone else, we trusted God to use their song to change the world in powerful ways?

Perhaps they will change us, too. After all, the challenging people in our lives are part of the melody God has given us to sing. Will we own that song and accept the way in which God desires to bring us blessing? Are we willing to help those people own the songs within them and find God's redemptive beauty there, even when it costs us? Let us be people who sing the stories of our lives with integrity and faithfulness, knowing that God is our composer. He will perfect our songs in His perfect time, just as He did for Rahab.

OUTSIDE THE LINES

1. *"Anyone who belongs to Christ has become a new person. The old life is gone; a new life has begun!" (2 Corinthians 5:17).*

a. It is easy to recall our past and feel regret. Yet Paul points out that when God redeemed us, He gave us a new vision. How can you uncover and then develop a new outlook on what's ahead for you or a loved one?

b. One verse before this passage, the apostle Paul says he has "stopped evaluating others from a human point of view." Consider a person in your life who struggles with disabilities or weaknesses. How do you think Christ views that person? How does reflecting on verse 16 alter the way you see him or her?

2. *"I waited patiently for the LORD to help me, and he turned to me and heard my cry. He lifted me out of the pit of despair, out of the mud and the mire. He set my feet on solid ground and steadied me as I walked along. He has given me a new song to sing, a hymn of praise to our God. Many will see what he has done and be amazed. They will put their trust in the LORD."* *(Psalm 40:1-3).*

    a. Undoubtedly Rahab waited years for her life to change. As a prostitute whose home was in the walls of the city, she lived on the outskirts of society both figuratively and literally. What circumstances have led you to desperately long for change? According to the psalmist, how should you wait?

    b. What is the payoff for waiting for God to answer your deepest longings? How have you or someone you know seen the Lord lift them from the pit?

What "new song" are you or that person now sharing with others?

3. *"Forgetting the past and looking forward to what lies ahead, I press on to reach the end of the race and receive the heavenly prize for which God, through Christ Jesus, is calling us" (Philippians 3:13-14).*

   a. If we remain caught in the remembrance of our mistakes, we will be unable to move forward. What are some ways that God has redeemed your past? Write them down and ask God to help you make that your focus.

b. What obstacles in your life keep you from seeking Christ? How would you describe our heavenly prize? How might meditating on that help you keep your focus on God?

CHAPTER 8

It Might Get Better, but It Isn't Going Away

*Each one has to find his peace from within. And peace
to be real must be unaffected by outside circumstances.*

MAHATMA GANDHI

Acceptance (noun)
1. the action of consenting to receive or undertake something offered
2. willingness to tolerate a difficult situation

*O Lord, you are a great and awesome God! You always
fulfill your covenant and keep your promises of unfailing
love to those who love you and obey your commands. But
we have sinned and done wrong. We have rebelled against
you and scorned your commands and regulations. We have
refused to listen to your servants the prophets, who spoke
on your authority to our kings and princes and ancestors
and to all the people of the land.*

Lord, you are in the right; but as you see, our faces are

covered with shame. This is true of all of us, including the people of Judah and Jerusalem and all Israel, scattered near and far, wherever you have driven us because of our disloyalty to you. . . .

O my God, lean down and listen to me. Open your eyes and see our despair. See how your city—the city that bears your name—lies in ruins. We make this plea, not because we deserve help, but because of your mercy.

O Lord, hear. O Lord, forgive. O Lord, listen and act! For your own sake, do not delay, O my God, for your people and your city bear your name.

DANIEL 9:4-7, 18-19

DANIEL: THE LONG-SUFFERING PROPHET

Daniel was dreaming again. He often dreamed; God had blessed him with visions that spoke to him, and often to others, of things to come. This dream, however, was of the distant past. He was walking along a wall next to the city gate with the night guards, waiting for dawn. He looked back into the city; it waited in tranquil slumber, unaware of the dangers outside the gates. It was his home, his beloved Jerusalem, housing the people of God's covenant. In his dream, Daniel turned back to the eastern horizon, just as the first light appeared over the rolling hills, toward Babylon.

He awoke suddenly. He was in his chambers in the house of Cyrus, king of Persia. It had been many years since his eyes had alighted on the sight he most longed to see, his beloved homeland of Judah. He had long been a prisoner of Persian overlords, a stranger walking through a strange land.

As a young man, when Jerusalem first fell and Daniel was taken on the long trip to Babylon, he was afraid. Many members of his family had fallen to the Babylonian sword, and only a few trusted friends remained with him. And yet as he passed through unfamiliar landscapes on his way to his new home, he remembered the words of the law and repeated them to himself over and over. When he arrived in Babylon, he was ready to face what awaited him in the great unknown of the future.

It didn't take long for Daniel and his friends to be thrust into the center of political intrigue. The conquering king, Nebuchadnezzar, was upset that his astrologers couldn't reveal the content and meaning of a troubling dream to him, so he threatened to have all of them executed. God revealed the dream and its interpretation to Daniel, who was rewarded by Nebuchadnezzar with great power and a position of leadership within Babylon. His stormy interaction with Nebuchadnezzar was only the beginning. He would go on to take part in the saga of the fall from power of a later king, Belshazzar. Later still, Daniel would be a political prisoner facing the threat of death under Darius, Belshazzar's usurper. Once again, God would raise him up and bring him to places of great authority and influence. He would be mightily blessed by God.

And yet even while recognizing God's favor, Daniel longed for his homeland. His heart hurt when he thought of the beautiful city of Jerusalem, now lying in ruins. His life had been brought to a place of blessing and goodness, but he knew that he would remain an exile for his entire life, never able to return to Judah.

Whenever he was tempted to despair, Daniel would remember the vision of things to come, given to him by an angelic messenger from God. Great turmoil and the rise and fall of nations, yes, but God would prevail in the end. Though he might not see the ultimate redemption accomplished by God's hand, he could trust that all would be put right one day.

So in the meantime, Daniel worked, dwelt in the land appointed to him, and worshiped God. Though Daniel was in exile, God wanted to bless him and use his life to change kings' hearts, and to proclaim God's ultimate plan to redeem all things.

Are you like Daniel? Are you facing a permanent difficulty that is with you day in and day out? Like Daniel, God sees you and wants to help you grow and live according to His kindness. There are several things to keep in mind.

It will get better, but it's not going away. When your world is unalterably changed and you face circumstances you never expected, it is normal and natural to grieve for the life you are leaving behind. If you can't grieve what has been lost, you won't be able to move on and accept God's plan for the future. God is close to the brokenhearted, and He also grieves for the brokenness of this world. God does not desire that we suppress the sadness permeating our lives; He wants to walk with us through those difficulties and bring us into the light of His redemption on the other side. The only way to do that is to recognize the darkness and look to your heavenly Father to illuminate the path in front of you.

It may not be going away, but it will get better. Daniel couldn't escape the stark fact that he would never see his native land again; yet God lifted Daniel up and fulfilled his desire for purpose and joy. By entrusting himself to the God who knows and cares, Daniel accomplished far beyond what he could have in his own capacity. God wants to do beautiful things in your life, no matter the circumstances you face. He is far bigger than your situation, and will do far beyond what you can imagine if you entrust yourself to Him.

The story God is telling through your life may be far better than you could possibly imagine. Would it have been natural for Daniel to feel sorry for himself and to keep his head down in the midst of his new circumstances? Certainly; however, by entrusting himself to God even in dire extremes, Daniel was raised to a place of power, and he became one of the most revered prophets in Israel's history. God was able to accomplish mighty things through Daniel, in spite of Daniel's circumstances. God wants to do the same for you; He has a plan for your life, and that plan can never be irredeemably derailed as long as you turn your heart back to God, in every circumstance and every change. Even in exile, He can bless you.

OUTSIDE THE LINES

1. *"Not that I was ever in need, for I have learned how to be content with whatever I have. I know how to live on almost nothing or with everything. I have learned the secret of living in every situation, whether it is with a full stomach or empty, with plenty or little. For I can do everything through Christ, who gives me strength"* *(Philippians 4:11-13).*

   a. According to this verse, contentment is a process. Name three areas where you struggle to accept your situation.

   b. How can you, like the apostle Paul, "learn" to be content? Make one goal for the next six months for the way in which you plan to practice being content in the difficult circumstances of your life.

2. *"True godliness with contentment is itself great wealth.
   After all, we brought nothing with us when we came into
   the world, and we can't take anything with us when we
   leave it. So if we have enough food and clothing, let us be
   content"* (1 Timothy 6:6-8).

   a. We live in a time when we are taught to want more,
      rather than to be happy with what we have. Name
      several ways in which God has provided for you,
      and thank Him for His faithfulness.

   b. It's easy to think that godliness should result in
      some great work in the world, but this verse seems
      to indicate that choosing to be content can actu-
      ally be our work of service to the Lord. Write down
      ways you intend to worship God through your
      contentment.

3. *"LORD, you alone are my inheritance, my cup of blessing. You guard all that is mine" (Psalm 16:5).*

   a. If your circumstances never change, how can you choose to see the blessing of God in the fabric of your life?

   b. The difference between living in despair and living by faith often comes down to a choice of our will to trust God and to see Him as our greatest prize. Daniel began his prayer in chapter 9 this way: "O LORD, you are a great and awesome God! You always fulfill your covenant and keep your promises of unfailing love to those who love you and obey your commands" (verse 4). Write a brief prayer that opens with your acknowledgment of how you've seen God at work in your life.

CHAPTER 9

It's a Marathon, Not a Sprint

*Endurance is not just the ability to bear
a hard thing, but to turn it into glory.*

WILLIAM BARCLAY

Endurance (noun)

1. enduring an unpleasant or difficult process or situation
   without giving way
2. the capacity of something to last or to withstand wear
   and tear

---

*One night Joseph had a dream, and when he told his
brothers about it, they hated him more than ever. "Listen
to this dream," he said. "We were out in the field, tying up
bundles of grain. Suddenly my bundle stood up, and your
bundles all gathered around and bowed low before mine!"*

*His brothers responded, "So you think you will be
our king, do you? Do you actually think you will reign*

over us?" And they hated him all the more because of his dreams and the way he talked about them.

Soon Joseph had another dream, and again he told his brothers about it. "Listen, I have had another dream," he said. "The sun, moon, and eleven stars bowed low before me!" . . .

So when the Ishmaelites, who were Midianite traders, came by, Joseph's brothers . . . sold him to them for twenty pieces of silver. And the traders took him to Egypt. . . .

Then Pharaoh said to Joseph, "Since God has revealed the meaning of the dreams to you, clearly no one else is as intelligent or wise as you are. You will be in charge of my court, and all my people will take orders from you. Only I, sitting on my throne, will have a rank higher than yours." . . .

After burying Jacob, Joseph returned to Egypt with his brothers and all who had accompanied him to his father's burial. But now that their father was dead, Joseph's brothers became fearful. "Now Joseph will show his anger and pay us back for all the wrong we did to him," they said.

So they sent this message to Joseph: "Before your father died, he instructed us to say to you: 'Please forgive your brothers for the great wrong they did to you—for their sin in treating you so cruelly.' So we, the servants of the God of your father, beg you to forgive our sin." When Joseph received the message, he broke down and wept. Then his brothers came and threw themselves down before Joseph. "Look, we are your slaves!" they said.

But Joseph replied, "Don't be afraid of me. Am I God,
that I can punish you? You intended to harm me, but God
intended it all for good. He brought me to this position so
I could save the lives of many people."

GENESIS 37:5-9, 28; 41:39-40; 50:14-20

JOSEPH: THE MAN WHO WOULD BE KING

It all started with a dream—the dream that told Joseph he
would be great. Someday, the stars themselves would bow
before him. Joseph knew the truth all too well from his
father: When God spoke and declared something to be, the
very sea itself couldn't turn back the tide of divine will. He
had the blessing of the God of his fathers, and his destiny was
sealed. His very family would bow before him as he governed
and stretched out his hand over all the land.

He tried to remind himself of this in the darkness of a
musty well, a prison made for him by his own brothers. He
spoke it into being as if it were a mantra as he was being
dragged out and sold into slavery in Egypt. He leaned on
it as a lifeline as he watched everything he knew disappear
over the horizon forever. To the unknowing eye, nothing
remained for him but the shame of servitude in a foreign
land. Even so, Joseph was patient; he believed that what God
had spoken over him in a vision would become a reality. He
planted the seed of this belief in the broken soil of his story
and began the long and arduous wait for God's revelation.

When he arrived in the household of Potiphar, Joseph

thought perhaps the first signs of bloom were coming up out of the ground. As the commander of Pharaoh's guard, Potiphar knew a man of greatness when he saw him. Joseph was no ordinary slave; there was a spark of vision there. Potiphar wasn't one to waste talent, and Joseph quickly rose to great power. Was this the Lord's meaning? Was this the culmination of the dream? Sometimes Joseph looked up at the stars and remembered his vision; no, it wasn't time yet. There was more to be done.

It didn't take long for this truth to become painful reality. Potiphar's wife, a woman jealous of her husband and angry at Joseph's favor, would have none of it. She knew how to shift hearts and minds; her husband might be commander of the guard, but *she* commanded her husband. She would show that sniveling Hebrew Joseph what true power looked like. Many greater men had fallen to her wiles, and Joseph would be an easy target.

However, Joseph proved more difficult to corrupt than she had first expected. Not to be deterred, she planned a special encounter, one she was sure Joseph wouldn't be able to resist. The setting was perfect; no one else was at home, and she used all her wiles to draw him into her spell. Despite her best efforts, and to her great rage, he walked away from her once again. From *her*! No one would defy her and get away with it; she grabbed his cloak as he tried to slip away, and ran to her husband, accusations of assault on her lips.

Joseph could have revealed all; he could have taken matters into his own hands. He was a trusted servant after all,

Potiphar's right-hand man. But Joseph trusted God's timing. Power was nothing if it came from anyone but God. As he was carted off to prison, Joseph laid his life at the feet of the God who had made a promise and who he believed with his whole heart would come through in the end.

More waiting; more trusting. And God once again showed his faithfulness to Joseph. Even in prison, Joseph found favor; his waiting was not in vain, nor was it wasted. God cultivated the soil of Joseph's life as Joseph put his trust in Him. This God, who had promised Joseph's fathers great triumph, had made the same promise to Joseph. He would not waver; he would not turn aside.

And suddenly, Joseph's vision became reality. God had given another man of greatness, Pharaoh himself, a vision. However, instead of offering a glorious promise, Pharaoh's vision was a nightmare, and even worse, inexplicable to him. Tortured by his thoughts, he sought help from the man God had prepared for two decades. It was time for God to use the man of vision to interpret a vision for another. And so Joseph was empowered by God to give to Pharaoh the understanding to heed the dream and take steps to protect his people. In gratefulness, Pharaoh himself, one of the greatest rulers in the world, bestowed upon Joseph a power beyond imagination, to rule over all of Egypt.

As Joseph looked out from his place of power, he considered the multitude of people over whom he had been given authority, like countless stars bowing before him. In time, his brothers would also come to bow before him, seeking his mercy as they fled a famine in their own land. Though the light of their stars was fading, Joseph repaid their evil with goodness. God always had a plan, and Joseph's dream had finally come true. The promise had finally bloomed into a beautiful array of divine faithfulness.

Have you been given a dream? What if the promise will be fulfilled through the very thing with which you most struggle? What if God wants to tell a great story through your different child, family member, or friend, and He has entrusted that person to you as a protector of that story? What if you are a steward of the dream God wants to blossom through this person?

God is a master gardener; He plants and cultivates, and He understands that flowers bloom only in the right season. Perhaps you aren't in the season for blooming yet; perhaps God still wants to cultivate the promises He has made to you. Put your trust in His understanding; His promises are true, and He will be faithful to them.

OUTSIDE THE LINES

1. *"Since we are surrounded by such a huge crowd of witnesses to the life of faith, let us strip off every weight that slows us down, especially the sin that so easily trips us up. And let us run with endurance the race God has set before us. We do this by keeping our eyes on Jesus, the champion who initiates and perfects our faith"* *(Hebrews 12:1-2).*

a. A runner keeps his eye on the goal. What is the goal God has given you to run toward?

b. Persevering over the long haul requires a great deal of training day by day. What character training might God have in mind for you in the midst of your present circumstances?

2. *"Dear brothers and sisters, when troubles of any kind come your way, consider it an opportunity for great joy. For you know that when your faith is tested, your endurance has a chance to grow"* (James 1:2-3).

a. Our culture gives us permission to compromise under pressure. But we are given more capacity than we think through the work of the Holy Spirit. In what areas are you tempted to compromise? Who or what causes you to despair that any good can come from your situation? Pray that God will give you the grace to expand your capacity beyond your ability.

b. Often we get caught up in the stress of the moment instead of seeing the bigger picture. The truth is, God sees farther than we do, and He is using our circumstances to make us into people of godly character. What characteristics do you want to define your life in the long term? Write these down and commit to seeking them in every circumstance.

3. *"For I know the plans I have for you,' says the LORD. 'They are plans for good and not for disaster, to give you a future and a hope'"* (Jeremiah 29:11).

a. Our hope in this life is based on the fact that God is good. What does this verse tell you about the character and plans of God?

b. Sometimes in the midst of our circumstances, we wonder if God is still leading us. Like Joseph, the people of ancient Israel, to whom this promise was first directed, had become exiles in a foreign land. Given the way they had failed Him, they certainly had reason to wonder whether God would come through on His promise. In what areas do you struggle to believe that God will come through for you? What lessons can you take away from Joseph's time in Egypt to remember God's faithfulness even on the darkest days?

CHAPTER 10

Give Yourself a Break

Most of the things we need to be most fully alive
never come in busyness. They grow in rest.

MARK BUCHANAN

Rest (verb)

1. cease work or movement in order to relax, sleep, or recover strength
2. allow to be inactive in order to regain strength, health, or energy

Elijah was afraid and fled for his life. He went to Beersheba, a town in Judah, and he left his servant there. Then he went on alone into the wilderness, traveling all day. He sat down under a solitary broom tree and prayed that he might die. "I have had enough, LORD," he said. "Take my life, for I am no better than my ancestors who have already died."

Then he lay down and slept under the broom tree. But as he was sleeping, an angel touched him and told him, "Get up and eat!" He looked around and there beside his head was some bread baked on hot stones and a jar of water! So he ate and drank and lay down again.

Then the angel of the LORD came again and touched him and said, "Get up and eat some more, or the journey ahead will be too much for you."

So he got up and ate and drank, and the food gave him enough strength to travel forty days and forty nights to Mount Sinai, the mountain of God. There he came to a cave, where he spent the night.

But the LORD said to him, "What are you doing here, Elijah?"

Elijah replied, "I have zealously served the LORD God Almighty. But the people of Israel have broken their covenant with you, torn down your altars, and killed every one of your prophets. I am the only one left, and now they are trying to kill me, too."

"Go out and stand before me on the mountain," the LORD told him. And as Elijah stood there, the LORD passed by, and a mighty windstorm hit the mountain. It was such a terrible blast that the rocks were torn loose, but the LORD was not in the wind. After the wind there was an earthquake, but the LORD was not in the earthquake. And after the earthquake there was a fire, but the LORD was not in the fire. And after the fire there was the sound of a gentle whisper. When Elijah heard it, he wrapped his

face in his cloak and went out and stood at the entrance of the cave.

1 KINGS 19:3-13

ELIJAH: THE EXHAUSTED PROPHET

Elijah was running again.

He always seemed to be running. He could remember the strength the Lord put into his legs, how they burned with power as he dashed beyond human speed ahead of King Ahab's chariot. He remembered the wind in his face, as if it were a challenge against the mission given him by the Living God. He welcomed it and pitched into the gust with spirited defiance. He had declared the Lord's word to Ahab—that a storm was coming after a long period of drought, and indeed the storm arose. But whereas Ahab fought the peril of the elements crashing down upon him, the storm had been at Elijah's back, enabling him to race home with mighty power.

Now, however, he was sprinting away from another storm, and he knew he wouldn't be able to outrun this one. It was, in one sense, a storm driven by the anger of Jezebel, the wife of Israel's King Ahab. She fell into a rage when she heard that four hundred priests of the idolatrous god Baal had been slain at Elijah's command. Whereas the true God had consumed an offering with blazing fire, the false god Baal had not shown up to set fire to the offering presented by the idol's desperate priests.

But it was more than this. Elijah had given his whole life

into the service of the Lord; he had fought valiantly against the foes of Jehovah, striking down idol worshipers and putting the fear of the Lord of hosts back into the hearts of the Israelite people. He had stood for righteousness in a time of great darkness. And yet as soon as one victory seemed sealed, the enemies of the Lord would surround Elijah and press down upon him again. No matter his efforts, the tide of disbelief, wickedness, and unfaithfulness rose up like a wave within the people of Israel, crashing down upon him in fury.

This time Jezebel had sworn to kill Elijah within a day's time, and the storm of despair was upon him once more. He felt the first drops of doubt splashing down as he fled the queen: What had he accomplished? What good had he achieved? Evil triumphed; a profane queen ruled on the throne and was using her puppet king Ahab to fuel the terror, destruction, and malice all about. The people were weak; nothing seemed to sway their hearts from their corrupt ways. Elijah's prophetic ministry was a failure. *He* was a failure. Jezebel would catch him eventually and execute him; God might as well let him die now and save him from such a fate. Finally, his fatigue caught up with his hopelessness, and he collapsed under the shelter of a broom tree, where he fell into a troubled sleep.

He opened his eyes; for a moment he was certain he was dreaming. An angel had touched him, and he felt a power rush through him like adrenaline. He started to rise, and then the weakness of his body fell upon him like a hammer. "Come and eat. Over here." The angel pointed to a flat rock only a couple of feet away. Suddenly filled with intense hunger and thirst, Elijah devoured the meal. When he was finished, he was filled with peace and immediately fell into sleep again.

He awoke with a start; the angel had roused him again. "Get up and eat some more, or the journey ahead will be too much for you." At first Elijah felt disoriented; the fog of his dark thoughts continued to hover and confuse him. Yet at the angel's command, Elijah took up food and water again. As he swallowed the final bite, he could feel his senses clearing. He knew what he must do; he gathered his things, and, strengthened by rest and nourishment, gained the energy to set forth on a pilgrimage to Mount Sinai.

After forty days of arduous travel, Elijah ascended the holy mountain, stopping to spend the night in a cave. There he found the Lord waiting for him. "What are you doing here, Elijah?"

Elijah had reflected on that question for over a month during his travels. He had so many questions; he didn't understand what the Lord was doing. "I have zealously served [you], but the people of Israel have broken their covenant with you, torn down your altars, and killed every one of your prophets. I am the only one left, and now they are trying to kill me, too."

God's reply was immediate. "Go out and stand before me on the mountain."

As Elijah waited near the mountain's peak, he suddenly heard a great upheaval. The earth beneath him began to sway violently, and the wind picked up ferociously around him. Without warning, a flame shot into view, swirling into a mighty firestorm. As the tumult raged all about him, Elijah thought about all his troubles—the treachery of Ahab, the wickedness of Jezebel, the people denying God and serving idols, and all the running he'd done trying to outpace the storm of his doom. Elijah sought God in the midst of the pandemonium around him, but God wasn't there. Elijah was filled with dread as the void of chaos surrounded him.

And then he was alone on the mountain again, the moonlight beaming down in placid curiosity. On a gentle breath of wind, Elijah caught a faint whisper. It was God, speaking with a still, small voice. Suddenly Elijah remembered the angel; he recalled the bread and water that replenished his body and the transcendent peace of the slumber into which he had fallen. Elijah understood; God wanted him to *rest*. He had been running, wrestling with these issues far beyond his control; he had lost perspective, lost hope. In the midst of that senselessness, God wanted to give Elijah the peace that a gentle whisper of assurance brings.

Soon after, God would send Elijah his partner in ministry, Elisha, to help carry his load and carry on his work.

Just like Elijah, we can become so caught up in the difficulties of our lives that we lose perspective and begin to burn out. In those moments, we may feel like nothing can possibly get better. We are tempted to ask why God won't help us fix things, why He won't put everything in order for us. It is exactly in those moments that God wants us to be still; not to try to find His will in the storms all around, but instead to rest in His peace. Sometimes in the midst of crisis we need to take a moment to pause and let the Lord minister to us. Sometimes the most godly thing to do is to fight the good fight; at other times the most godly thing to do is to sleep, to receive nourishment through food and drink, and to wait on the Lord instead of struggling to find answers on our own.

Let the Lord who is the king over all storms put His peace in your heart today.

OUTSIDE THE LINES

1. *"Be still in the presence of the LORD, and wait patiently for him to act. Don't worry about evil people who prosper or fret about their wicked schemes"* (Psalm 37:7).

   a. As he ran from Jezebel, Elijah struggled because he was focused on fear of what could be rather than on God's presence and provision in the moment. When you face opposition or outright evil in the midst of your struggle, are you more prone to wait patiently on God, to worry about others' motives, or to fret about the harm they are doing to you? What can you learn from Elijah about how to persevere, even when others come against you?

b. Define three practical ways you can build rest into the midst of the craziness around you.

2. *"Remember to observe the Sabbath day by keeping it holy"* *(Exodus 20:8).*

   a. Why did God call us to keep the Sabbath holy? How does our rest honor Him and help us?

   b. Many intrusions, from social media to phone calls to TV, interrupt what could be peaceful moments of our lives. What distractions keep you from rest? What is one way you could diminish the noise this week?

3. *"Then Jesus said, 'Come to me, all of you who are weary and carry heavy burdens, and I will give you rest. Take my yoke upon you. Let me teach you, because I am humble and gentle at heart, and you will find rest for your souls'"* (Matthew 11:28-29).

   a. Sometimes we think we need to do something spiritual or godly to approach God, when in fact, Jesus invites us to come as we are. Take a few minutes to come to Jesus right now, naming each burden you set down before Him.

b. Jesus was speaking to people who'd had heavy
demands placed on them by the religious leaders
of their day. Why is God's way better? How does
this verse show Jesus' concern for the weary?

CHAPTER 11

Don't Beat Yourself Up

*God never tires of forgiving us; we are the
ones who tire of seeking his mercy.*

POPE FRANCIS

Mercy (noun)

1. kind or forgiving treatment of someone who could
   be treated harshly
2. kindness or help given to people who are in a very bad
   or desperate situation

---

*After breakfast Jesus asked Simon Peter, "Simon son
of John, do you love me more than these?"*

"Yes, Lord," Peter replied, "you know I love you."

"Then feed my lambs," Jesus told him.

*Jesus repeated the question: "Simon son of John, do you
love me?"*

"Yes, Lord," Peter said, "you know I love you."

"Then take care of my sheep," Jesus said.

A third time he asked him, "Simon son of John, do you love me?"

Peter was hurt that Jesus asked the question a third time. He said, "Lord, you know everything. You know that I love you."

Jesus said, "Then feed my sheep." JOHN 21:15-17

PETER: THE FALLIBLE ROCK

It was second nature to him. Peter loved fishing with friends in the early morning, before the sun had come up; it was as familiar to him as breathing. He relished the feel of the thick, woven nets in his coarse hands, each strand slipping between his fingers, and the resistance as he heaved them into the waiting boat. He took comfort in the cool of the water splashing up his arms, a welcome respite from the heat that hovered like a blanket, even in the predawn hours.

Peter especially loved fishing because it brought to mind the best moment of his life; the moment Jesus called him to ministry. These nets, with which he had wrangled all his life, had led him to an encounter with the living God. He had never been the same, learning how to love others and usher them into God's Kingdom, as the Master called it. He was as good at persuading people of the gospel as he was at catching fish; Jesus even fondly called him a "fisher of men," a title in which he took great pride. Because of Peter's new life with Jesus, ministry left little time for fishing, but whenever the opportunity arose for a free morning on the Sea of Galilee, he would jump at the chance.

This morning, however, was different. He had hoped that fishing, which had always relaxed him, would be a welcome diversion from the nightmare of the previous days; he had even brought a number of friends, including James, John, Nathanael, and Thomas, along for company. Instead, every tug at the empty nets and every rock of the boat back and forth was a cruel reminder of the life that had been given him, the life he had so quickly and carelessly thrown away. He had denied the Master—not once, but three times. As his Lord was led off to be crucified, Peter had protected himself behind a veil of lies, rejecting everything that might cause him harm. In the terror of that night, the lies had come as naturally as breathing, but then he remembered what Jesus had said. Deep sorrow overwhelmed Peter at the memory of Jesus telling him that he would deny his Lord before the cock had finished crowing to announce the coming of the morning.

Yes, of course the fact that Jesus had been resurrected from the dead was a miracle beyond believing. Everything he and all Jesus' followers had hoped for had been confirmed; a new world had begun. But not for Peter. He still felt as if he were on the outside looking in, watching the festivities but unable to participate. Jesus couldn't use him now; he had messed up the one thing he had been given to do—to follow Jesus no matter the cost. Now the memory of that cock crowing taunted him mercilessly, each crow another reminder of who Peter was: failure, liar, traitor.

Peter was pulled out of his brooding by the faint sound of a voice from the shore. The figure calling out was too far away to see, but he could clearly hear the man asking if they'd caught any fish.

When one of the men on the boat shouted no, the stranger said, "Throw out your net on the right-hand side of the boat, and you'll get some!"

Peter's heart leapt within him; the stranger's words shocked his memory awake, and he remembered the first time he had heard those words, when Jesus had called him to ministry so long ago. Surely this time, though, it was all some sort of cruel joke, a prank to make fun of his disgrace. Surely nothing good could come of following the stranger's instructions; and yet what did they have to lose? Peter was already humiliated beyond imagination. Why not go along with the ruse?

Several of the disciples took the nets and tossed them over the side. Almost immediately, they were thrown off balance as the boat tipped sideways. The water bubbled up furiously as thousands of fish began jumping to the surface and filling the net. As they drew it into the boat, Peter looked at John, who was beaming. "It's the Lord!" John said, delight drawn all over his face. Peter couldn't believe it; could history really be repeating itself? The smallest spark of hope lit within him, and before he could think, he had thrown on his outer garment and dived into the water, furiously swimming to shore.

When Peter arrived, dripping, on shore, he felt ashamed

all over again. Here he was, unprepared to meet his Master, wet and sloppy like a fool. But Jesus just smiled at him and invited him to sit by a waiting fire. As the others rowed the boat to shore, they found Jesus roasting them all a delicious breakfast. When everyone was settled down and Peter had enjoyed a few bites of the delectable meal, Jesus motioned for him to follow, and the two walked along the shore, away from the fire and from prying ears.

After a while, Jesus stopped and looked Peter straight in the eyes. "Simon, do you love me more than you love these?"

Almost out of habit, Peter replied, "Yes, Lord, you know I love you."

"Then feed my lambs." Jesus set back to walking again in silence, His head angled down thoughtfully. After a few minutes, He stopped and said it again. "Simon son of John, do you love me?"

A knot started to form in Peter's throat. Jesus had called his bluff; somehow He knew Peter's answer had been half-hearted, careless. Here he was, the problem child all over again, caught red-handed by his Lord. But he did love the Master; he so longed for Jesus to know that he loved Him. If only Jesus could know how much he wanted to do the right thing, to please Him.

"Yes, Lord, you know I love you." He said it almost as if pleading with his Master to believe him.

"Then take care of my sheep."

Jesus stopped and repeated the expected words. "Simon, son of John, do you love me?"

From Peter's subconscious rose up the crow of the rooster. Failure; liar; traitor. Over and over again. Three words, three denials of his Lord. And now the Lord was asking him whether he loved Him for the third time. The agony of shame rose up within Peter, and he began to understand. He had given away his honor, his righteousness, betraying the only One he truly loved; and here was Jesus, freely giving back that which was most precious to him, that which Jesus had every right to hold against Peter. What could Peter's love mean in the face of this sort of love? His was a meaningless love, even if it was honest.

Hurt filled Peter's heart, and tears welled in his eyes. "Lord, you know everything. You know that I love you." He bent his head in sorrow and sat dejectedly on a rock.

Jesus, stooping to His knees, lifted Peter's chin. "Then feed my sheep."

For the first time that day, Peter truly understood. His love could never have earned him Jesus' approval because he would always be prone to falling. It was only because of his Master's grace that Peter's desire to do the right thing could ever be accomplished. Jesus wanted him to "feed [His] sheep," not because Peter would never make a mistake, but because his love for Jesus was sourced first in Jesus' love for him. Only in that power could Peter live and die for God. Peter stood, restored to ministry, and walked anew into his redeemed life.

Maybe you know someone who just can't seem to get it right. Maybe you're that person. If so, God wants you to know something: You are justified by Him. Of course you will fail; we all fall down eventually. You may even betray Him by turning your back on Him when He doesn't answer your prayers the way you want or by lashing out at someone who has hurt you or threatens you. But your failures define you only if you focus on them instead of your Savior. It is in His power and through His kindness that you are able to do good and fulfill His purposes for your life. Let the burden of your own guilt drop away and entrust yourself to the God who can give you true forgiveness.

OUTSIDE THE LINES

1. *"There is no condemnation for those who belong to Christ Jesus" (Romans 8:1).*

   a. According to this verse, how much condemnation does God feel toward us when we make mistakes?

   b. To think we will never sin or fall again is unrealistic. Write down three ways you feel you have failed.

Then write this verse over the list of failures you have written down. Finally, throw the list away, knowing that God's grace is immediate and His forgiveness everlasting.

2. *"Most important of all, continue to show deep love for each other, for love covers a multitude of sins"* *(1 Peter 4:8).*

   a. Peter made decisions he regretted throughout his life, even after he was placed in leadership in the church. Yet his love for others had its source in Jesus, who forgave him and enabled him to persevere in the work to which Christ had called him. Why do you think love is so critical to moving past the ways we sin against one another?

b. If God has forgiven you infinitely, there will never be a point at which you can stop forgiving others. Name the people in your life who need your unconditional love today, and write down three ways you can show that love to them.

3. *"Now go and learn the meaning of this Scripture: 'I want you to show mercy, not offer sacrifices.' For I have come to call not those who think they are righteous, but those who know they are sinners" (Matthew 9:13).*

a. We try to get people to change using all sorts of methods—from giving them the silent treatment to giving them a lecture. Yet according to this Scripture, true influence comes through humility and mercy. Why should we extend such grace to others, even when we think we are in the right?

b. Name three people in your life who need your
   mercy. Define one specific way you will extend God's
   mercy to each of them this week—for example, by
   writing a note, giving a gift, or spending meaningful
   time with them.

CHAPTER 12

Misfits for the Kingdom

*The kingdom is not an exclusive, well-trimmed suburb
with snobbish rules about who can live there. No, it is
for a larger, homelier, less self-conscious caste of people
who understand they are sinners because they have
experienced the yaw and pitch of moral struggle.*

BRENNAN MANNING

Hope **(noun)**

1. a person or thing that may help or save someone
2. grounds for believing that something good may happen

*Every year Jesus' parents went to Jerusalem for the Passover
festival. When Jesus was twelve years old, they attended the
festival as usual. After the celebration was over, they started
home to Nazareth, but Jesus stayed behind in Jerusalem. His
parents didn't miss him at first, because they assumed he was
among the other travelers. But when he didn't show up that
evening, they started looking for him among their relatives
and friends.*

When they couldn't find him, they went back to

Jerusalem to search for him there. Three days later they finally discovered him in the Temple, sitting among the religious teachers, listening to them and asking questions. All who heard him were amazed at his understanding and his answers.

His parents didn't know what to think. "Son," his mother said to him, "why have you done this to us? Your father and I have been frantic, searching for you everywhere."

"But why did you need to search?" he asked. "Didn't you know that I must be in my Father's house?" But they didn't understand what he meant.

Then he returned to Nazareth with them and was obedient to them. And his mother stored all these things in her heart.

Jesus grew in wisdom and in stature and in favor with God and all the people. LUKE 2:41-52

JESUS: THE ONCE AND FUTURE KING

Mary and Joseph were frantic. Everything had seemed to be going so well; they had gone up to Jerusalem for the Passover, as they did every year. Afterward, they headed back to Nazareth. When they set out, Mary assumed that Jesus must be playing with the other children; but after a quick search, it became apparent that He was absent from their traveling party.

Anxious and irritated at having to enter Jerusalem again—

and feeling somewhat mortified by having to explain to their family and friends why they were turning back—Mary and Joseph finally found themselves at the Temple, not knowing what else to do. It was often like this with Jesus; they had known from the beginning that Jesus was special, sent from God as the Messiah. They were chosen for a special task and felt deeply honored to have been given such a stewardship. And yet there were moments when it was so hard to understand Jesus' ways. He was like any other child in appearance and in His desire to please His parents, but Mary knew from the beginning that His heart ultimately was led by something far beyond her comprehension.

From somewhere above them, they suddenly heard Jesus' voice rise above the noise of the city. Running up the stairs of the Temple, they saw Jesus speaking, surrounded by several rabbis. When Jesus saw them, He paused for a moment. Mary broke the awkward silence. "Son, why have you done this to us? Your father and I have been frantic, searching for you everywhere."

It was then that Mary and Joseph realized something: The religious leaders were staring at Jesus in awe, as if they were marveling at Him. These well-educated men were listening to their son and learning from Him.

Jesus replied, "But why did you need to search? Didn't you know that I must be in my Father's house?"

When the trio finally departed Jerusalem to catch up with their caravan, Mary marveled at Jesus' words. He was calling the Temple His Father's house, speaking with such intimacy about something so unapproachable for many. *He always has marched to the beat of a different drummer*, thought Mary. Now, however, she understood who the drummer was, and it made all the difference in the world.

When it comes to people in Scripture who bucked the trend, Jesus is our prime example. He was unfazed to see men dismantling the roof above Him so He could perform a miracle for their friend. He refused to live by the book and offended many people—even the powerful religious leaders—with His strong words. He lived life to the fullest, celebrating with food and drink so much that the religious leaders around Him called Him "a glutton and a drunkard." He randomly cursed fig trees and intentionally blessed lepers, touching those who were allegedly untouchable. He hung out with frauds and prostitutes, preferring their company to the high and mighty. He constantly got into trouble with the authorities, unapologetically healing the sick on the Sabbath and angrily trashing the Temple courts. He ended up dying a criminal's death on a cross, and He defied death by rising again in glory. He turned the world upside down and showed us that living a misfit life is the way into the Kingdom.

You see, Jesus loves misfits; they're the people He uses to change the world. Those who have it all together are too busy to be bothered with the messy, beautiful life of God's Spirit. The imperfect, the weak, the ones who struggle with not fitting in, or who can't seem to ever get it right already know their own fallibility. God doesn't want perfect people;

He wants humble people, people who say "I'm pretty messed up and can't fix the world in my own power. It's You or nothing, God."

In the end, of course, we're all misfits—some of us are just better at hiding it than others. It's easy to look at friends and family who struggle with a learning disability or depression, or who are too loud, or who keep making mistake after mistake, and think, *At least I've got it more together than they do.* The truth is, if the Lord is ever going to use any of us, it will be only after we are able to look at ourselves and admit our own fallenness. Only then will we have nothing to lose. Only then will we ask God to come into our lives and make us misfits for His Kingdom.

When we go to church and share in the Communion table, we are feeding on Jesus. Through His sacrifice on the cross, we are fed by Him; not by anything else in our lives, but truly by our Lord, who transforms us through His powerful presence in us. At the table, everyone is made equal; everyone from the president down to the homeless guy who wanders in off the street. Through our human eyes, we see people as well-dressed or sloppy, as composed or out-of-control, as polite or too loud. We see wealth and status, and we look at people with obvious disabilities differently from those who seem to have it all together.

At the table, Jesus wants to give us His eyes so we can look at everyone around us not through the lens of their outward appearance but through the lens of Christ living within them. Looking through that grid, every one of us is a misfit in the world of winners and losers, saints and sinners. Yet at the same table, we step out of the box of condemnation and into the free air of the Holy Spirit transforming us.

Those misfits in your life? They are your way of seeing Jesus a little bit more clearly; they show you a God who wants to free you from guilt, failure, frustration, and the strain of unreal expectations. Perhaps you feel like coal that is being squeezed by pressure beyond what you think you can handle. You are afraid that what you are will be lost; perhaps in a sense this is true. You will lose the right you thought you had to certain fundamental expectations in your life; you may lose a sense of comfort and entitlement. But the good news is that the diamond you are being shaped into is far more beautiful than the carbon you leave behind. While the superficial things of life—your status, your wealth, your comfort, your rights, the career you wanted, the family you had expected—may slip away, your essence—the person at your very center that God created you to be—will come into beautiful clarity, perhaps for the first time in your life. And maybe you'll even see that those superficial elements were imperfections getting in the way of God's desire to transform you.

Today, as you struggle to understand and affirm the misfits in your life, or if you are an outlier yourself, embrace Jesus' call to be like Him—a misfit in this broken world, pointing to a Kingdom where everyone has a place and is made beautiful.

OUTSIDE THE LINES

1. *"It is impossible to please God without faith. Anyone who wants to come to him must believe that God exists and that he rewards those who sincerely seek him"* *(Hebrews 11:6).*

Use the following space to journal about what God has taught you as you've journeyed through the lives of twelve people in Scripture who were misfits. As you ponder your own life story, in what ways do you desire to see God work in your circumstances through eyes of faith?

ABOUT THE AUTHORS

SALLY CLARKSON has a heart for mentoring women. Inspiring them to live intentional and meaningful lives as they engage in God's love and purpose is the driving force of her multifaceted, international ministry. Since founding Whole Heart Ministries (WholeHeart.org) with her husband, Clay, she has inspired thousands of women through conferences, podcasts, her blog, and the many books she has written, which include bestsellers like *The Lifegiving Home* (with Sarah Clarkson), *Own Your Life*, and *Desperate* (with Sarah Mae).

As the mother of four, Sally advocates tirelessly for the power of motherhood and the influence of home through her Mom Heart ministry (MomHeart.org). She often speaks to audiences worldwide and promotes the formation of support-group Bible studies to encourage women in many cultures. Online, Sally encourages many through her blogs and websites—SallyClarkson.com and LifegivingHome.com—as well as through her e-books and live webinars.

If you are interested in finding a Mom Heart group in

your area, use the contact form at MomHeart.org. You can find information on upcoming events at SallyClarkson.com.

JOEL CLARKSON is an award-winning composer who is known for the vibrant colors of sound he paints with his music, from the soaring, cinematic sounds of his film music to his melodic, pensive piano works. Joel's composition is often focused on film scores, and he has provided original music for numerous feature and short films in addition to orchestrating and conducting for many different genres and settings. He has also received high praise as a concert composer and orchestrator, and his creative contributions to concert music have been heard around the world to great acclaim. Joel has provided his expertise in many other artistic environments as well, including the audiobook world, where he has delighted listeners near and far as an engaging voice artist, and also in nonfiction publishing, where he has collaborated as a creative contributor and editor on multiple bestselling books. Joel was born in Vienna, Austria, and received his undergraduate degree from the Berklee College of Music, summa cum laude. He and his mother, Sally, are also the coauthors of *The Lifegiving Home Experience*. He currently finds his home in the shadow of the beautiful Rocky Mountains in Monument, Colorado. For more information, please visit JoelClarkson.com.

NOTES

NOTES

NOTES

NOTES

NOTES

NOTES

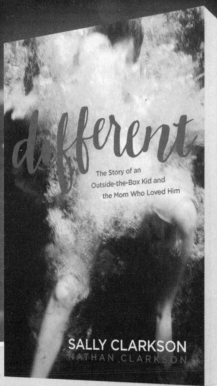

Books by Sally Clarkson

OWN YOUR LIFE

THE LIFEGIVING HOME
(with Sarah Clarkson)

THE LIFEGIVING HOME EXPERIENCE
(with Joel Clarkson)

DIFFERENT
(with Nathan Clarkson)

A DIFFERENT KIND OF HERO
(with Joel Clarkson)

THE MISSION OF MOTHERHOOD

THE MINISTRY OF MOTHERHOOD

YOU ARE LOVED BIBLE STUDY
(with Angela Perritt)

DESPERATE
(with Sarah Mae)

Visit her online at SALLYCLARKSON.COM.

CP1190